# HE LEADS ME

*"Faith over Fear"*

He Leads Me: "Faith over Fear"

ISBN 978-976-96975-0-8

Unless otherwise indicated, all Scripture quotations are taken from the Holy Bible, New International Version®, NIV®. Copyright © 1973, 1978, 1984, 2011 by Biblica, Inc.™ Used by permission of Zondervan. All rights reserved worldwide. www.zondervan.com. The "NIV" and "New International Version" are trademarks registered in the United States Patent and Trademark Office by Biblica, Inc.™

Scripture quotations marked (MSG) are taken from The Message. Copyright © 1993, 1994, 1995, 1996, 2000, 2001, 2002. Used by permission of NavPress Publishing Group.

Scripture quotations marked (AMP) are taken from the Amplified® Bible (AMPC), copyright © 2015 by The Lockman Foundation. Used by permission. www.lockman.org.

Scripture quotations marked (AMPC) are taken from the Amplified® Bible (AMPC), copyright © 1954, 1958, 1962, 1964, 1965, 1987 by The Lockman Foundation. Used by permission. www.lockman.org.

Scripture quotations marked (KJV) are taken from the King James Version, which is in the public domain in the United States.

Edited by: Gina Mushynsky and Dr. Janice Jules

Cover Design by: Aspect Creative
Telephone: 1 (246) 255-7654
Instagram: @AspectCreative

Interior Design & Layout by: Shelev Publishing
Telephone: 1 (246) 257-9611
Instagram: @ShelevPublishing

# Acknowledgements

All praise, honor, and glory to my Lord and Savior Jesus Christ for saving and loving me and without whom this devotional would not have been possible.

Thanks to my husband, Andrew, my biggest cheerleader and encourager (he believes in me when I don't believe in myself). He's always quick to say, "You can do it."

Thanks to my mother, Eileen, who encourages, nurtures and worries, but believes in my abilities. Thanks also to my "other mothers," Denpha, the late Glendene and Monica—avid supporters and encouragers who love and loved me as though they birthed me.

Special thanks to my extended family and friends who have loved and supported me through the years and throughout this journey. My spiritual sisters and darling friends Dorian, Sophia P, Denise, Natasha, Sophia A and by extension my entire prayer team and church family.

Special mention to Gaynelle Corbin, author of Returning to My First Love, whose encouragement was integral to me reaching this milestone. Your guidance and advice with this process was invaluable.

To Gina Mushynsky for copyediting and Dr. Janice Jules for proofreading this manuscript, thank you both for lending your expertise to this book.

Thanks to Jean-Luc Applewhite of Aspect Creative, who took my vision and brought it to life in a beautiful book cover.

# Contents

# Introduction

I wrote these devotions five years ago, when I endured a season of losing my voice for about seven weeks. In that period of distress, I took the time to engage with God about an issue that plagued me perennially — fear! I purposed that God, and I would tackle this issue as I girded myself with the weapon that He gave us - His Word. So, I searched for those Scriptures that deal with fear and began the journey. It was during that time that these devotions were birthed. It's amazing what God uses to fulfil His purpose in us!

Today, I am thankful that I have grown by leaps and bounds— not that there aren't instances where I might feel fearful, but I am more confident in the truth of who I am and that I am victorious through Christ Jesus.

As you read, I pray that you would be encouraged to know that you too, can be victorious if Christ is at the center of your life. I also want to encourage you that if you don't know Him as Lord and Savior, choose Him today and have access to Faith over Fear.

# *Day 1*

## Courage in the Face of Fear

**Bible Verse:** Joshua 1:9 *"Have I not commanded you? Be strong and courageous. Do not be afraid; do not be discouraged, for the Lord your God will be with you wherever you go."*

I'm sure that there are many instances in life when we feel afraid (trust me, I know it well). This could happen because of a job loss and being fearful of what the future holds, having a new assignment and being fearful of failing, or dealing with the possibility of losing a loved one due to illness.

There will always be some instance or circumstance which might bring fear into our spirit. However, as we see in today's Bible reading, God commands us not to fear. Four commands are presented in this Scripture:

1. Be strong

2. Be courageous

3. Do not be afraid

4. Do not be discouraged

These commands come with a promise: that "the Lord your God will be with you wherever you go."

We are reminded that God never leaves us nor forsake us, and that when we go through something, He's right there with us; we're never alone. So, the next time you're facing a situation that brings you fear, remember Joshua 1:9 and know that your Father is right there with you.

*Dear God, thank You for being an ever-present Father. Help me to be strong and courageous, and to trust that You are always there with me. In Jesus's name. Amen*

# Reflection:

# Day 2

## Hope in the Lord

**Bible Verse:** Isaiah 40:31 *But those who hope in the Lord will renew their strength. They will soar on wings like eagles; they will run and not grow weary, they will walk and not be faint.*

The *Concise Oxford English Dictionary* defines hope as "expectation and desire combined for a certain thing to occur; a person, thing or circumstance that gives cause for hope ... a feeling of trust." It also indicates that it is something in which we are confident.

Hope in the Lord includes certain guarantees or promises, as illustrated in the verse above:

1. The promise of renewed strength.

2. The promise that you will soar on wings like eagles.

3. The promise that you will run and not grow weary.

4. The promise that you will walk and not grow faint.

However, these promises are predicated on having our hope in the Lord. When we do, we avail ourselves of these great promises.

God didn't promise that the Christian walk would be an easy one. But oh, what hope we have in Him! When we face circumstances that seem bigger than ourselves, or seem overwhelming or insurmountable, when we feel weak, we are reassured that if we hope in Him, he will give us the strength to carry on.

Oh, the promise of soaring like an eagle:

That we can rise above every circumstance if we hope in Him.

That we have the strength to run this race triumphantly; that as we hope in Him, though we might feel weary, we will be able to endure to the end.

That we will walk boldly, not growing faint, as He walks alongside us.

*Father, I thank You that You are the Lord of hope. Today I put my complete hope in You and trust You will renew my strength and help me to soar, to not grow weary or grow faint.* In Jesus's name. Amen.

# Reflection:

# Day 3

## You Will Not Be Consumed

**Bible Verse:** Isaiah 43:2 *"When you pass through the waters, I will be with you; and when you pass through the rivers, they will not sweep over you. When you walk through the fire, you will not be burned; the flames will not set you ablaze."*

Oh, how glorious is our God! Get a vivid picture in your mind of wading through floodwaters and rivers, the gushing waters consuming you. There are instances in life when we feel that we are drowning in the everyday demands of life, such as chores, work, children, marriage and family. Every area of our lives feels like we're in deep waters, far out to sea, unable to swim or save ourselves. But glory to God! The Word assures us that we have a mighty lifeguard who will be with us when we pass through the waters and rivers. He won't let us drown, but will keep us afloat, safely above the waves.

Similarly, when you encounter testing, the "fire" that seems to be consuming you, the situation that feels that it's going to kill you or suck the very life out of you, where there appears to be no way out— a hostile work environment, a wayward or rebellious child, a broken marriage, beloved family members who refuse to acknowledge God, a life-altering illness or injury, or a betrayal— whatever it may be, God's Word encourages us that we will NOT be consumed. We will come out unscathed.

Just as He was with Shadrach, Meshach, and Abednego, He will be with us in the fire and we shall not be burnt. Just like the Israelites, we shall pass through the waters if we place our complete trust and faith in Him.

*Thank You, God, that You are mighty to save us when we can't save ourselves. Thank You for being with us in every storm and fire in our lives and promising that if we continue to trust You and to hope, we shall not be consumed.* In Jesus's name! Amen.

*Reflection:*

_____

_____

_____

_____

_____

_____

_____

_____

_____

_____

_____

_____

_____

_____

# Day 4

## Encourage One Another

**Bible Verse:** 1 Thessalonians 5:11 *Therefore encourage one another and build each other up, just as in fact you are doing.*

The Message version expands on the above Scripture: "So speak encouraging words to one another. Build up hope so you'll all be together in this, no one left out, no one left behind. I know you're already doing this; just keep on doing it."

It's difficult to encourage someone else when you're feeling discouraged. However, this verse clearly states that we should encourage each other. Jesus was the greatest encourager that ever lived, and the Holy Spirit dwells within us; therefore, we have the power to be great encouragers as well to our brothers and sisters.

This verse challenges us to take the focus off ourselves and to think about others. I have personally experienced being discouraged while still encouraging others, oh what joy it is! I have found that in being selfless and encouraging others, I too have been encouraged. As it says in the Message version, "Build up hope so you'll all be together in this"; we share the burden together, thereby fostering hope.

Recently, I viewed a video that examined our reaction to news (gossip) and the pressing need to share that news. It cautioned that we should use three filters: *truthfulness, goodness,* and *usefulness.* If the news is not truthful, good, or useful, then it's not worth sharing. The Word tells us that the power of life and death lies in the tongue. Let us use our words to uplift others, to speak words of love, hope, comfort, peace and joy.

Today, use your words intentionally to bring hope, to inspire and to influence others so that no one feels alone or left behind.

*Lord, thank You that You are the encourager of my soul. Help me to be conscious of what I say and that my words would always be used to encourage and to reflect Your love, for Your glory.* In Jesus's name. Amen

*Reflection:*

_____

_____

_____

_____

_____

_____

_____

_____

_____

_____

_____

_____

_____

_____

_____

_____

# Day 5

## Trust in the Lord

**Bible Verse:** Proverbs 3:5–6 *"Trust in the Lord with all your heart and lean not on your own understanding; in all your ways submit to him, and he will make your paths straight."*

If you're like me, you're a fixer: one who tries to figure things out and come up with solutions to fix the situation or problem. But this is not limited to my situations. I like to fix situations for others too! Yeah! Sometimes that approach works and situations are fixed, sometimes only temporarily. However, in some cases they are not fixed at all.

I've found that the issue is that during those times of my fixing, I trusted in myself and leaned on my own understanding: my knowledge, wisdom, prior experience, skills, etc.

But as the above verse illustrates, we need to trust God with *all* of our hearts, not some of our hearts. That denotes *all* the way in! It doesn't mean "You take this part, Lord, and I'll do the rest." No! It means complete trust in Him; not trusting in ourselves or our abilities but leaning completely on Him.

In *all* of your ways submit to Him. Give Him lordship over every situation: release it all to Him. I've found that when I submit situations to God, they've worked out far better than I could have imagined. He works it (or them) out for us that trust Him completely and love Him wholeheartedly. We have the assurance in the Word that He *will*, not might or maybe, but *will* make every crooked path straight.

So be encouraged that you can trust God completely to make the impossible, possible; the dark, light; the sorrow, joy; the broken places, healed; and the dry places, flow with streams. You don't have to do it on your own, because we serve a limitless God; and if you trust Him, submit to Him, and follow His precepts, He will make your paths straight.

*Father, I thank You that I don't have to figure it out on my own. I thank You that I don't have to fix everything, but I can trust and submit it to You, the great FIXER. I thank You, trust You, love You, lean on You, and submit it all to You.* In Jesus's name! Amen.

# Reflection:

# Day 6

## Take Heart

**Bible Verse:** John 16:3 *"I have told you these things, so that in me you may have peace. In this world you will have trouble. But take heart! I have overcome the world."*

Many of us are familiar with Darlene Zschech's song "Victor's Crown." We sing lustily that Jesus has overcome the world. But in our everyday lives, are we living as though Jesus overcame? Are we trusting that in every situation, the victory is already won? The enemy is defeated, and we are victorious?

I'm not going to pretend that this is my posture or default in every situation and I'm sure I'm not alone. The Word clearly states that trials and tribulations will come, as we say, "in all shapes and sizes." However, the command is that we should have a posture of peace.

The Message version of today's Scripture verse aptly states, "I've told you all this so that trusting me, you will be unshakable and assured and deeply at peace." This means trusting Him with an unshakable, unmovable faith because Jesus has already done it for us.

We need not fear, but instead have peace in the midst of the storms of life. You may sway but you won't break. Jesus will hold you up; He will carry you through, He will comfort you through and He will love you through. If you trust in Him and have peace you will certainly overcome. So whatever you're going through today, take heart! God's got this! You've already won!

*Thank You, Lord, that through faith and peace we have victory in You. Help us to always trust in Your peace and assured victory.* In Jesus's name. Amen.

*Reflection:*

# Day 7

## Safe Place

**Bible Verse:** Psalm 46:1–3 (MSG) *God is a safe place to hide, ready to help when we need him. We stand fearless at the cliff-edge of doom, courageous in seastorm and earthquake, Before the rush and roar of oceans, the tremors that shift mountains. Jacob-wrestling God fights for us, God-of-Angel-Armies protects us.*

Where do you run and hide? What's your safe place? To whom, what, or where do you go to seek refuge? Is it a friend, spouse, family, or alcohol; a place to think, to be alone, to vent, to cry; or is it the safest place that you can ever run to—the arms of God?

We're reminded in this verse that God is a (*the*) safe place, always ready to help when we need him. We're encouraged that we can stand fearless against any peril. This is vividly illustrated with the reference to natural disasters in today's Scripture but could refer to any storm that we are facing in our lives. However, we're told that we can be courageous; put more succinctly, "We need not fear." God is with us *always*.

Get a clear vision in your mind that the God of heaven and earth, the God of angel armies is fighting for you. Nothing coming against you shall prosper. What storm, hurricane, earthquake, or disaster in life can defeat you? None can stand against the power of God. So, get excited! Be confident that heaven's armies are fighting for you! Victory is yours!

*Father, I thank You that You are my safe place. Thank You that I never have to face anything alone and that You are always fighting for me. Help me to always acknowledge You as my safe place and to run to You first.* In Jesus's name. Amen.

# Reflection:

# Day 8

## Love as God Loves

**Bible Verse:** Luke 6:35 *"But love your enemies, do good to them, and lend to them without expecting to get anything back. Then your reward will be great, and you will be children of the Most High, because he is kind to the ungrateful and wicked."*

It's easy to love people who love us; however, this verse urges us to love our enemies. What! Love those who hate you or me? Yes! That's what we are called to do. Furthermore, we are commanded to *actively* love them. This involves doing good for them and giving to them without expecting anything back.

Surely it would be so easy to do these things for someone you love, but not an enemy. Not a person who betrayed you, hurt you, took from you, or mistreated you.

But ah! God assures us that it is worth it and that there's a reward for this obedience. This reward extends beyond this world. It's not for earthly gain, but for the eternal reward with God himself.

We're also reminded that we too are sinners and despite our shortcomings, our God is gracious and loving toward us. He loves us when we are hateful and unloving. *He loves us!*

Therefore, just as God loves us through our mess, we should extend the same love to those who are unloving toward us. So today, remember that the ultimate love is God's love. It is His desire that we love each other as He loves us.

*Father, thank You for Your endless love. Help us daily to love others, especially our enemies, as You love us.* In Jesus's name. Amen.

# Reflection:

# Day 9

## Step onto the Water

**Bible Verse:** 2 Corinthians 5:7 (MSG) *It's what we trust in but don't yet see that keeps us going.*

I want you to imagine stepping out and walking on water. I'm sure you're probably saying, "Are you crazy?" If you grew up in Barbados, you are familiar with the saying "The sea ain't got no back door." Simply put, if you go out too far there's no coming back; there's no escape route. When you think about the sea, all you see is miles and miles of water that seem to have no end.

I don't know about you, but growing up, based on that old saying, I ventured as far into the sea as I could stand comfortably. If I couldn't stand, that meant it was too far and that it was time to retreat closer to the shore. (I'm sure I'm not alone in this thinking, even today).

However, trusting in God calls us into deep water. It requires us to exercise faith. Though it seems crazy to others, wading into the depths demonstrates total trust in Him. I used the analogy of the sea to allow you to catch a vision of walking hand in hand with God and knowing that as you walk, your faith and trust in God—even in rough seas—will keep you safe.

The seas will not overtake you; you are safe in your Father's arms. No harm or danger shall overtake you. The trust that I'm talking about goes beyond where you can stand.

I used the sea as an illustration, but you may be facing many different situations in your life. Whatever you're facing, don't be afraid: step boldly, knowing that your God has got you! Just as you can't see the end of the sea, you're probably not seeing the end of your situation. You're consumed and worried about how it will turn out. However, as the verse says— keep going, exercise your faith in what you cannot see and trust in our God who will make it all clear and who knows the outcome.

*Father, we come to You today and ask that You help us to strengthen our faith. Help us to walk fearless upon the water; full of faith of who You are.* In Jesus's name. Amen.

# Reflection:

# Day 10

## Stand

**Bible Verse:** Ephesians 6:13 *Therefore, put on the full armor of God, so that when the day of evil comes, you may be able to stand your ground, and after you have done everything, to stand.*

This verse encourages us to put on God's armor so that we can stand when the day of evil comes. It doesn't say *if*, but *when*; there is a surety that the day will come, but we have the assurance that when that day comes, we have access to be outfitted with the full armor of God.

The chapter goes on to outline what the armor consists of: the belt of truth, the breastplate of righteousness, the gospel of peace, the shield of faith, the helmet of salvation, and the sword of the spirit (the Word of God). God assures us that we can stand against anything if we have the armor on. These weapons are not man made, but spiritual, as we are reminded that we do not fight against flesh and blood but against the rulers, against the authorities, against the powers of this dark world..." Thus, our enemy is not a mortal one.

Our wonderful Father is always concerned about us and He ensures that we are always taken care of. He, the ultimate defender, equips us with weapons in which we can make a stand against the enemy. We have many battles to fight in this life, but the Word says that we are overcomers. So, trust that if you put on the full armor of God, you *will* be able to stand and when you have done all —to *stand*.

*Father, thank You for your provision. Thank You that we have access to your armor to stand when the day of evil comes. Help us to always trust in Your protection and the strength of Your armor.* In Jesus's name. Amen.

*Reflection:*

# Day 11

## It's Possible

**Bible Verse:** Mark 10:27 *Jesus looked at them and said, "With man this is impossible, but not with God; all things are possible with God."*

I have a sheet set from the "Sleep on the Word" line with that verse on it. It is comforting and a constant reminder that I need not be dismayed because nothing shall be impossible for and with my God.

So often we become discouraged because we try to solve problems and challenges on or own. We try to do them in our own strength and as a result, we either quit before we start to tackle something; stop midway through or fail because we thought we could do it by ourselves.

However, if we involve God from the onset, we can be sure that the situations will seem less overwhelming and can be accomplished, if we do it with God's help and with His strength.

Therefore "I can't" will become "I can with God's help." "I'm not equipped" will become "I am equipped through Christ Jesus." "I'm not strong enough" will become "I can with God's strength." "I don't know" will become "With God's wisdom I will know." So, think on these things the next time that you are discouraged or trying and failing in your strength. Lean upon God and know that what is impossible for you is not impossible for your heavenly Father.

*Father, thank You that we can draw on Your strength, Your wisdom, and Your love. Help us to know that nothing shall be impossible for us with You on our side.* In Jesus's name. Amen.

*Reflection:*

_____

_____

_____

_____

_____

_____

_____

_____

_____

_____

_____

_____

_____

_____

_____

# Day 12

## Draw on His Strength

**Bible Verse:** Isaiah 40:29 *He gives strength to the weary and increases the power of the weak.*

Lately, or for the past few weeks (although it seems like forever), I've been having issues with my throat and voice. There are some days when I feel very weary and other days when my mind is willing, but my body just does not have the strength.

Illness in the body can make us feel that way, but sometimes life itself can become wearisome. We can become weary working, taking care of children and home, exercising, and even in doing good.

Oftentimes when our bodies feel weary, we reach for a pick-me-up (mine is a Tiger Malt, *a local malt beverage*). Others might go for their favorite energy drink or shake. While these things might work in the moment, the Word points us to a timeless, limitless source of power.

When we are weary, we can draw on the strength of the Lord. The above verse says He gives it to us and that He increases our power. While worldly fixes are temporary and offer momentary strength, God's power is sustaining and available to us, His children.

So, when life's trials weigh you down, not only physically but spiritually, and you're feeling weary and worn, know that there's a power from which you can draw.

*Lord, thank You that Your strength and power are available to us. Help us to always turn to You first when we feel weary, trusting that we will be strengthened and powerful.* In Jesus's name. Amen.

# Reflection:

# Day 13

## Our Help

**Bible Verse:** Psalm 121:1–2 (AMPC) *I will lift my eyes to the hills [around Jerusalem, to sacred Mount Zion and Mount Moriah]—From where shall my help come? My help comes from the Lord, Who made heaven and earth.*

Today's Scripture is a popular verse that has been set to music and at some point in our lives we likely would have sung the familiar refrain (*I'm sure you're singing along with me at this point*). Even though we might know the verse and sing the chorus, there are times when our first response is not to look to the maker of heaven and earth.

For sure, I am guilty of this. I might first turn to a friend or my husband and *then* consult God. However, over time and more recently I have chosen God as my first response or "first responder."

We have earthly first responders. We call an ambulance when we have emergencies that merit a trip to the hospital, the fire department to deal with fires, and the police to deal with criminal matters.

Unlike earthly first responders, we, the children of God, have a first responder (our God) who is always on call, never late, and always available to us. Therefore, without hesitation we should look to Him, our very present help in times of danger, our strong tower, our defender, our protector, our all-in-all— God. Hence, I urge you to trust in the Lord, the maker of heaven and earth, our great source of help in every circumstance.

*Lord, I thank You that we can look to You as the source of our help. Help us to always turn to You first.* In Jesus's name. Amen.

*Reflection:*

# Day 14

## Wait with Confident Expectation

**Bible Verse:** Psalm 27:13–14 *I remain confident of this: I will see the goodness of the Lord in the land of the living. Wait for the Lord; be strong and take heart and wait upon the Lord.*

The Amplified Bible sums it up clearly: "I would have despaired had I not believed that I would see the goodness of the Lord in the land of the living. Wait for and confidently expect the Lord; be strong and let your heart take courage; yes, wait for and confidently expect the Lord."

If you receive an email from me, you will see the NIV translation of that verse at the bottom. Over a year and a half ago, a friend and sister in Christ sent me a word of encouragement along with that verse; it was just what I needed at that moment in my life. I was so moved and encouraged that I immediately used it as the signature on my emails.

On many occasions since then, I have had to turn to that verse and remind myself that though situations seemed impossible, sometimes dim, and gloomy, sometimes hopeless; where it seemed as though no goodness could be realized, like David, I, Roberta *(and you could insert your name as well*), will see the goodness of the Lord in the land of the living. Thus, while I am still alive, I will see and experience God's goodness. I can surely testify that I have indeed experienced His goodness.

Verse 14 encourages us to wait upon the Lord. Yes! I know waiting can be difficult, especially when you're desperate and need breakthrough *now*. However, the verse doesn't say to wait passively; it says be *strong* and take *courage* and *confidently expect*. Therefore, you must really believe that God will come through for you. He will prove himself, so we must always be expecting it to come to pass with upmost confidence.

It might take some time, but God's timing is always perfect and if we're believing and confidently expecting, we *shall* see His goodness.

*Father, thank You for Your faithfulness to us. Thank You that we can confidently and with sure expectation, wait upon You as Your goodness comes to pass in our lives.* In Jesus's name. Amen.

# Reflection:

# Day 15

## You're Valuable

**Bible Verse:** Matthew 6:26 *"Look at the birds of the air; they do not sow or reap or store away in barns, and yet your heavenly Father feeds them. Are you not much more valuable than they?"*

Have you ever really taken the time to study the behavior of birds; to observe how they gather dry grass and sticks to make a nest for their young ones? If you've ever fed them by giving them bread or scraps of food, you concede that you've fed them on some occasion; however, most of the time they thrive on their own without our assistance.

We might pay more attention to birds if they were to enter our home, build a nest close to our dwelling, or worse, commit the unforgivable sin of "messing up" our car! Then, for sure, we would acknowledge the presence of the birds.

This verse brings into sharp focus the care and love that the heavenly Father has for the things He created. It reminds us that birds don't work (they don't have a 9 to 5); they don't plant and reap food, yet God takes care of their needs. He makes sure that they are taken care of, fed, and sheltered.

Consider, then, that you are created in the image of God. If He so cares for the birds, you who are created in His likeness are very valuable to Him. He will surely provide for your every need. We need not worry; we simply need to trust Him at His Word.

Trust Him with everything—your health, job, family, bills, cares, worry —*everything*. He *can* handle it. He *can* take care of it! He will ensure that His most valuable creation will not go wanting. He who did not even spare His own son for us—what wouldn't He do for you?

So, the next time you're tempted to worry about where the next meal will come from, how you will pay this or that bill, or take care of your children, know that you have a God who thinks the world of you: a God who considers you valuable. Just as He takes care of the birds, He will surely take care of—and do much more—for you.

*Father, thank You for the surety we have in You. Just as You take care of the birds, we thank You that You will do much more for us. We thank You and bless You.* In Jesus's name. Amen!

*Reflection:*

_____

_____

_____

_____

_____

_____

_____

_____

_____

_____

_____

_____

_____

_____

_____

_____

# Day 16

## Give Thanks

**Bible Verse:** 1 Chronicles 16:34 *"Give thanks to the Lord, for he is good; his love endures forever."*

Growing up, from as far back as I can remember, I was taught to say thanks. Granted, "thanks" was most likely limited to when I received something from someone. As I grew older, I understood that saying and giving thanks extended beyond the receipt of something tangible such as a gift.

Giving thanks extended to receiving a kind word or encouragement, being alive, and gratitude for the people in my life, for reaching goals, for jobs, and for good and bad experiences. Just thankful!

When I received Christ as my personal Savior, and as I grew more and formed a deeper relationship with Him, I understood "thanks" in a whole new way. Thanks for Christ dying on the cross for me! Thanks for Him being in my life; thanks for Him being with me every step of the way —every day. Thanks for Him loving me and chastising me; thanks for Him being in the valleys I encountered—and for the mountaintops too! Thanks for Him being God. Oh, so truly thankful!

God is worthy of praise, if only for our rising and seeing the sun, the sky, the grass; creation in all its glory— being able to breathe, see, smell, touch, and love. God is good, and His loving-kindness endures *forever*! That means forever and ever. His love never fails; it's eternal. So, open your mouth, lift your hands, and give thanks. Hallelujah!

*Father, thank You for Your enduring, eternal love. Thank You for Your goodness, even when we think we don't deserve it. Today I give thanks and praises to You.* In Jesus's name. Amen!

# Reflection:

# Day 17

## Unspeakable Joy

**Bible Verse:** 1 Peter 1:8 (AMP) *Though you have not seen Him, you love Him; and though you do not even see Him now, you believe and trust in Him and you greatly rejoice and delight with inexpressible and glorious joy.*

A customary greeting I received in the morning reminded me of that old chorus, "Joy Unspeakable," that I sang while growing up in my neighborhood Church of God assembly. It immediately brought a smile to my face as the lyrics ran through my head. I reminisced about beating cymbals (tambourines) and drums, and lustily singing the chorus that seemed to have no end. Oh, those were good days! Great, joyous memories!

We experience joy when pleasurable things happen. We celebrate life, birth, marriages, promotions, and accomplishing goals, to name a few. These time-limited joy moments last but a while, but we who know Christ have a lasting joy. The Word proclaims, "The joy of the Lord is your strength" (Nehemiah 8:10).

Though we haven't seen Jesus, we love Him, trust Him, and with great joy we anticipate meeting Him. This joy is fueled by faith and the knowledge that we are saved and received salvation of our souls. Joy in the Lord transcends the trials of life; it endures, since we have hope in Christ Jesus. It is not affected by happy or sad moments; instead, it is the joy that sees Christ in everything.

*Lord, we thank You for Your unspeakable joy that is unaffected by our circumstances. We greatly rejoice and delight in Your inexpressible and glorious joy.* In Jesus's name. Amen.

*Reflection:*

# Day 18

## Sing His Praises

**Bible Verse:** Psalm 105:1–2 (AMP) O give thanks to the LORD, call upon His name; Make known His deeds among the people. Sing to Him, sing praises to Him; Speak of all His wonderful acts and devoutly praise them.

Give thanks to the Lord, for He is indeed good! He is a good God, loving and faithful Father, comforter, redeemer, restorer, provider, healer; He is peace, love, hope, joy, protector, vindicator, sustainer, and preserver of life. He is awesome, marvelous, majestic, wonderful. He's so wonderful; that's what Jesus Christ is to me.

Let us shout His praise with a loud voice. Let's proclaim what He has done for us. We are called to share our testimonies of how God saved us, loved us, called us His own. Let us share with others the good news of His gospel!

Even on our bad days, we can still rejoice in the Lord, in His faithfulness and goodness toward us. I'm sure that you can recall many instances of God's goodness and faithfulness in your life. So let us fill the atmosphere with songs of praise to our God, for He is worthy of praise. Hallelujah!

*Thank You, God, for the opportunity to praise You. We count it a privilege and proclaim that no rocks will cry out in praise, but we will loudly and triumphantly sing Your praises.* In Jesus's name. Amen.

# Reflection:

_____

_____

_____

_____

_____

_____

_____

_____

_____

_____

_____

_____

_____

_____

_____

_____

_____

# Day 19

## Count It All Pure Joy

**Bible Verse:** James 1:2–3 *Consider it pure joy, my brothers and sisters, whenever you face trials of many kinds, because you know that the testing of your faith produces perseverance.*

Joy, joy! "Joy unspeakable and full of glory" (1 Peter 1:8 KJV). When I think of joy, I think of pleasant things, things that bring peace, happiness, smiles, contentment, good emotions, just sweet things, and moments.

Yet in this portion of Scripture, the opposite is proffered. It says count it *pure joy* when you face trials. Errggg! Trials = joy; therefore, trials produce joy? The computation is not immediate, nor does the equation seem to make sense. It seems like an oxymoron. How can one be happy or joyful during a situation that's ripping them apart, that threatens their sanity, that feels like there's no coming back from this? It just doesn't make sense to be joyful at some of the most painful moments of life.

However, we are instructed to face the trials with joy. Choosing joy leads to a result, which is perseverance. Perseverance speaks to being steadfast and a constancy in the pursuit of something.

Count it all pure joy! How different would it be if we face trials with a smile, like this, "Trial, how are you today?" "I'm joyful; let's go!" That would be the ideal, but so often we fall short. We resort to complaining, feeling down and depressed, or feeling like we're not in the will of God. But God is never far away from us.

Something is being worked out in us during the trial; we're developing skills that lead us to maturity when we face issues of life with joy. So today, as you face many trials, try joy as a first response. Put on joy, know that the trial has a purpose, and joy your way through!

*Father God, thank You for Your Word. Thank You for instructions on how we should respond to trials. Thank You for Your joy that is our strength, and we pray that You will help us to remember to count it all joy.* In Jesus's name. Amen

# Reflection:

# Day 20

## Seek God First

**Bible Verse:** Matthew 6:33 *"But seek first his kingdom and his righteousness, and all these things will be given to you as well."*

My girlfriend and I made a commitment to meet up for prayer seven days out of each month. However, over the past two months, life intervened and we have not been as consistent as we should be. One day, the Lord rendered us a stern rebuke and we have since recommitted our covenant, confessed our sin, and sought forgiveness. We are prayerfully pursuing this commitment.

While talking before prayer, my friend remarked that Mark 6:33 came to her, and the portion that stood out was "Seek first his kingdom and his righteousness," with a major emphasis on seeking God's kingdom *first!*

We revisited this portion of Scripture during our prayer time that morning, and it lingered in my spirit long after we were finished. I took up a notebook that I had written in about three weeks earlier while attending a monthly prayer meeting. We broke into pairs during the session, and before approaching the sister I was paired with, I wrote down her name and the words "Seek me, says the Lord; seek ye first the kingdom of God and His righteousness and these things will be added unto you." I smiled and called my friend; it's amazing how God confirms His word. I don't normally write in that notebook and have not taken it up since that night three weeks prior. I just *love* God!

The verses that precede today's Bible reading speak about worry. They urge us not to worry about what we would eat, drink, or wear, and assure us that our heavenly Father knows that we need these things. We are encouraged to focus our attention on the kingdom of God FIRST. Here is a simple way to remember the word first.

Foremost

Initially

Right up front (or Right at the beginning)

Singly (for He is Second to none)

Top of the list.

*First!* Seek first not a friend or the world, but *His kingdom* and His righteousness.

*His* righteousness, not man's righteousness. God's righteousness. This means seeking to be in relationship with Him and living according to His will and recognizing that justice and righteousness are the foundations of His throne. As believers, we have a covenant relationship with God; He's faithful to His Word. So let us strive to seek Him first always and to live a life that is pleasing to our heavenly Father.

He offers us the condition: seek His kingdom first and His righteousness, and *all* these things (everything we need) will be added to us.

*Father God, thank You for Your Word. Thank You that You are a loving and gracious Father. Help us to always seek first Your kingdom and Your righteousness.* In Jesus's name. Amen!

# Reflection:

# Day 21

## Search Me

**Bible Verse:** Psalm 139:23–24 *Search me, God, and know my heart; test me and know my anxious thoughts. See if there is any offensive way in me and lead me in the way everlasting.*

One morning I got the urging in the spirit to read Psalm 139. I picked up my Bible and started to read, then allowed distractions throughout the day to hinder me from doing so. On another morning, again I had the same urging; however, this time I stopped and intentionally sat and read it—and oh, what a revelation! As usual, I made copious notes, and out of those multicolored pen markings and jottings, verses 23 and 24 struck a chord in me, or rather, pricked me.

"Search me, God" speaks of surrendering, opening to God fully, recognizing that it is not what we think of ourselves or the good that others say about us, but coming to a place of surrender and confessing "search me, God, and know my heart." The heart is important. The Word tells us in 1 Samuel 16:7 that man looks at the outer appearance, but God looks at the heart. Looks are deceiving, but the heart shows our true intentions. We're also encouraged in the Word to guard our hearts, for everything we do flows from it (Proverbs 4:23).

The verse continues to say, "Test me and know my anxious thoughts." Earlier verses tell us how God knitted us; therefore, He knows us intimately. That means He knows what we are thinking, feeling, and going to say even before we do. Therefore, our posture should be "Search me, God," not "I'm good, so I don't need your approval, Lord. Everyone thinks I'm so sweet, so friendly, kind, and giving." We're none of us perfect, and I'll be the first to admit that sometimes I can be very self-righteous. I can do things or say things that hurt others and then justify my actions, still believing that I'm good natured. Therefore, if there's anything in me that offends you, Lord, reveal it; make me aware; convict me. I humbly seek your forgiveness, Lord.

David goes a step further and says, "Lead me in the way everlasting." It's not enough for us to be aware of our offenses; we need to be willing to be led by God and to say, "Forgive me, God! Walk with me today. I want to be better than I was yesterday, to lean not on my own understanding and to daily seek Your righteousness, not mine. I want to recognize that life is not about the world's approval but serving and pleasing You and living according to Your will and purpose."

*Father God, thank You for the revelation in Your Word. Thank You that You love us enough to chastise us. I pray that I would seek You for daily renewal and count it a privilege to come to You, my Creator, to search me, to know my heart, to test me, to reveal anything that is not of You, and to lead me in the way everlasting.* In Jesus's name. Amen.

# Reflection:

Printed in Great Britain
by Amazon

16575563R00054